girls' guide to wine

Susy Atkins

girls' guide to wine

MITCHELL BEAZLEY

girls' guide to wine

by susy atkins

This book is for my sister, Jenny.

First published in Great Britain in 2002 by Mitchell Beazley, an imprint of Octopus Publishing Group Limited, 2–4 Heron Quays, London E14 4JP.

Reprinted 2002, 2003 (four times), 2004, 2005, 2006

A CIP catalogue record for this book is available from the British Library.

ISBN: 1 84000 682 X

The author and publishers will be grateful for any information which will assist them in keeping future editions up-to-date. Although all reasonable care has been taken in the preparation of this book, neither the publishers nor the author can accept any liability for any consequences arising from the use thereof, or the information contained therein.

Commissioning Editor Hilary Lumsden
Executive Art Editor Yasia Williams
Illustrator Yadzia Williams
Managing Editor Emma Rice
Editor Jamie Ambrose
Production Alix McCulloch

Typeset in Lucida Sans, Helvetica, and Troubadour
Printed and bound by Mackays Ltd in the UK

Contents

why every girl needs this book

The range of wine
dilemmas that
most girls face

Why is this a GIRLS' guide to wine? Why not just have one for everybody? Well, clearly there are various reasons why women have a harder time than men when it comes to getting to know wine.

First,

men seem to think we have no taste.

That's the only explanation for the pathetic whites and rosés they have palmed off on us for years in wine bars and at dire parties. Until recently, we were complete martyrs in this respect and smiled far too easily when presented with a jug of lukewarm, oxidized gnats' pee.

Unsurprisingly, many of us have now decided that enough is enough. We want better wine – only that means getting to know more about it. So here are the basic facts: no-nonsense, down-to-earth, and as easy to absorb as a chilled glass of Sancerre.

Let's hope that, in the future, it is women who sit with a delicious glass of vino in the local bar, while a man (who hasn't had the advantage of reading this great book) sips something akin to the liquid that collects in the toilet-brush holder and tries to simper politely. You never know...

Second,

girls obviously have different needs when it comes to wine.

Girls want to know the cheapest wine to party with, the perfect wine for a dinner date, the best bottle for matching with seared tuna and a tossed salad. Let's face it: we *care* – and most men don't. They just want to get plastered and show off.

Talking of which, it's important to remember not to drink too much. Women cannot tolerate as much alcohol as men and should drink only a couple of small glasses of wine per day. And don't go skipping your allocation for a few nights and saving up eight glasses for Saturday – it doesn't work like that. (Actually, I only wrote this so that if some pious relatives are wondering whether to buy this for you, they might see it and decide that this is a sensible book. But, just so you know, there IS a chapter on "the morning after" which could come in handy.)

Some of the wine dilemmas solved in these pages – how to read a wine label, how to minimize the chances of being ripped off, when to cause a stink in a restaurant – are important ones. Others, such as how to avoid red-wine-and-lipstick stains, how to spot a wine bore a mile off, or how to spit wine at your toes in the bathtub, are obviously much MORE important. And the tips on wine drinking and dieting are, without doubt, more crucial than the meaning of life.

So, girls: welcome
to the wonderful world of wine!

So you REALLY wanna know about wine? Here's where you learn about the best grape varieties, the most important styles, and the best moments to crack a bottle open. This is the most serious part of an otherwise rather fluffy book. So: pay attention! (Or skip to the next chapter if you only bought this for a laugh.)

one step ahead

The world of
wine styles and
grape varieties

White Wine

The world is awash with CHARDONNAY – so much so that you'd sometimes think there was no other white wine available. The shops are simply stuffed with Chardonnay, restaurants are overflowing with it, and it's coming out of our ears at every party in town. There's this strange myth that all girls adore Chardonnay for its fruity, fun appeal, but I happen to know lots who don't like the mega-oaky types that leave you with a mouthful of sawdust. Understandably.

Also, there are lots of girls secretly wondering, "What on earth IS Chardonnay? Is it a brand name, a winery, a wine region, or an especially prolific winemaker – a Mr or Ms Chardonnay who is out there producing most of the globe's white wine?" Of course, they never dare to ask such an obvious question.

This book acknowledges these poor, misguided souls, and is here to set them straight once and for all. Chardonnay is a grape variety, OK? It's a type of vine, most famous as the grape behind the wonderful, life-enhancing drink that is white burgundy, from France. Almost all white burgundy is one hundred per cent Chardonnay, even though the name of the grape does not appear on the label.

The top white burgundies from some spots such as Meursault, Puligny-Montrachet, and Chassagne-Montrachet are arguably the best Chardonnays in the world: elegant, rounded wines packed with apples, peaches, oranges, cream, toasted nuts, toast... Phew! Sorry. Felt faint there for a moment.

Plenty of creamy vanilla

Chablis is another, especially hip, white burgundy – again, one hundred per cent Chardonnay. It can be a little lighter in style, more steely and refreshing – but don't count on it: most good white burgundy is pretty rich. But then, that's Chardonnay for you.

Examples from the South of France, Australia, and California are the most powerful of all: ripe and fruity, and with plenty of creamy vanilla and toasty oak if they've spent months ageing in barrel. If you don't like oaky Chardonnay, pick one that says it is lightly oaked or unoaked on the label (doh!).

Drink Chardonnay with food rather than by itself.

Its bold, fruity character gives it the wow factor with salmon, roast chicken, pasta in creamy sauces, barbecued fish....

Quality

Five to ten out of ten

Fashion statement

Was running high, now losing its trendy appeal. But will remain popular.

some Sauvignons have a whiff of tom-cat and male armpits

As we get a bit tired of Chardonnay, SAUVIGNON BLANC is swinging into fashion. In fact, Sauvignon (nothing to do with Cabernet Sauvignon) is suddenly VERY cool. Expect leaner, zestier, more mouthwatering flavours than Chardonnay, heading towards grassy in some cases (as in the Loire Valley, where Sancerre and Pouilly-Fumé are made from one hundred per cent Sauvignon, or Bordeaux, where it's blended with Sémillon to make dry and sweet wines), OR ripe and bursting with baked gooseberry and asparagus (New Zealand).

Sauvignon can be a bargain: the cheaper ones are a bit more watery and less exciting, but still refreshing and crisp. It's a great grape, all in all, even if it is a teeny-weeny bit predictable. And even though some Sauvignons have a whiff of tom-cat and male armpits about them (sexy? I'm not sure...).

Drink as a wake-up call to the senses,
or buy cheapies as party wines, or serve as a
great match for grilled white fish, salads, tomatoes,
and green vegetables like fennel or asparagus.

Quality rating
Four to nine out of ten.

Fashion statement
Definitely moving up in the world.

Then there's RIESLING. No, don't run away! Come back here! Riesling may be well and truly out of vogue, but it makes some of the best white wines in the world, and it deserves a lot more credit. Poor old Riesling gets blamed for lots of poor German whites, but it rarely appears in the truly terrible ones. Instead, it is responsible for some wonderfully refreshing, appley white wines that age very well, turning all honeyed and aromatic with age. Give it a try.

German examples can be dry (*Trocken*) or riper and somewhat sweeter (*Spätlese*) or they can be transformed into truly luscious dessert wines (*Beerenauslese* or *Trockenbeerenauslese*). Alsace, in eastern France, and Austria both produce good Rieslings, too. And the New World has joined the club by producing riper, lime-drenched Rieslings. Australian Riesling, all suntanned and rich, is well worth a whirl.

Drink dry Riesling as an elegant aperitif,

or pair it with fish, light oriental dishes, salads.
Try sweet Riesling with desserts or blue cheeses.

Quality rating

Six to ten out of ten.

Fashion statement

Was woeful, now possibly picking up. Could even become deeply groovy by, oh, the time we get too old to care.

Here's a bunch (geddit?) of contenders: PINOT GRIS, CHENIN BLANC, SEMILLON, and VIOGNIER. Pinot Gris, a.k.a. Pinot Grigio from Italy, can be appealing, rich stuff, terrific with food, but some Pinot Grigio is pretty insipid (a slightly pathetic, girly drink if ever there was one; make spritzers with it).

Chenin Blanc from South Africa makes acceptable everyday "glugging" wines, while serious Loire Valley Chenin can be much more refined and expensive. Think freshly chopped apples and limes with hints of walnut and honey.

Sémillon creates wines that are tart and lean when young, but fatter and richer when older (a bit like some of us). Try Australian ones.

A nice change from Chardonnay, Viognier is very much in vogue. This is a grape that, in the right hands, makes wonderfully perfumed, peach- and apricot-packed whites. It can also be dilute, flabby, and disappointingly bland if badly handled. Avoid the cheapest.

Think freshly chopped apples and limes with hints of walnut and honey

Red Wine

CABERNET SAUVIGNON. What can I say? Cab is fab! It is blended with Merlot in Bordeaux to make the famous châteaux reds (avoid the cheap ones, but splurge on a top example once in a while if you can). It's also grown – mainly for blending with other grapes – in Italy and Spain. Here, as well, it makes some top wines. It is a big hit in Australia (either solo or blended with Shiraz), Chile (by itself: great stuff – think pure cassis), California (serious, concentrated Cabernet for long ageing), and Argentina. Even drinking cheapies from the South of France and Eastern Europe isn't a bad way to while away an evening.

What's so marvellous about it? Well, try this: Cabernet makes long-lived, well-structured, deeply coloured wine with loads of juicy, sweet blackcurrant and ripe, blackberry flavours upfront, followed by layers of fresh mint, eucalyptus, chocolate, leather, cedar... serious red.

An all-round, smug, superior kind of a grape, Cabernet still has its flaws. It can be a little one-dimensional, so it's often blended with other varieties to "fill in the gaps". And it's rarely an easy-going, party wine. It is well-structured, full-bodied – tough, even. So it needs food.

Crack Cabernet open
with red meat, strong cheeses, and hearty stews.

Quality rating
Five to ten out of ten.

Fashion statement
Immortal. Cabernet seems immune to trends.

If Cabernet rises above mere fashion statements, MERLOT does not. A few years ago, Merlot was considered something of a hanger-on, the blending partner with Cab in Bordeaux reds. Now it's as cool as a dip in the Atlantic. Everyone is mad about Merlot, especially in America, where Merlot-mania is running riot. It's not hard to see why. This is a grape that produces super-fruity wines oozing ripe, red berries and squashy plum flavours. It's medium-bodied (so fairly easy to enjoy by itself, but still good with food); it's vibrant, supple, plump, and fleshy. Yum, yum, YUM!

Merlot still plays an important part in Bordeaux reds (the wines of St-Emilion and Pomerol are mainly Merlot, with a bit of Cab thrown in). In fact, more Merlot is grown in France than any other red grape. It's not always tasty, though; bottles from the southwest (Bergerac, Languedoc) vary in quality – so watch it. Elsewhere, light, slightly grassy Merlots are made in Italy; fine examples come from New Zealand and South Africa; and concentrated, chunky Californian ones are among the best. Chilean Merlot is juicy and good value.

Drink with

roast beef or roast chicken, stews, good cheeses, goose, turkey...

Quality rating

Three to ten out of ten (but avoid cheapies).

Fashion statement

Off the scale. As hip as De Niro in his heyday. Or Mike Myers in *Goldmember*, depending on your point of view.

PINOT NOIR is another groovy grape, and it always has been. Especially among top winemakers who would do anything, but anything, to make great wine from such a difficult vine. This is the soft, strawberryish red that creates burgundy; expect silky, ripe, perfumed, seductive stuff when the wine's young, then more funky, earthy, leathery, even vaguely horsey character when it's older. Yep, it's sexy stuff. Unless you pick a dud, which is quite easy.

Pinot IS tricky for even a talented winemaker to handle, and its wines can be thin, tart, dilute and dull. If you want to taste GOOD Pinot, you'll have to shell out for it. Some cheap Chileans are OK, but the best from France, California, New Zealand, and Oregon will make your credit card tremble in fear. Embark on a Pinot passion with care.

Drink light Pinot Noirs

with salmon or tuna; richer ones with duck, game, or squishy, soft cheeses.

Quality rating

Three to ten out of ten.

Fashion statement

Such a sexy wine could never be passé.
Crack it open at romantic moments.

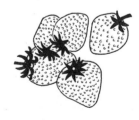

dense, with chocolatey depths

For fans of rich, spicy, blockbuster reds, there's nothing quite like SYRAH. Or SHIRAZ, as it's known in Australia (and some other places where they deliberately try to confuse you). Syrah is Very Important in the Rhône Valley in France, where it makes top reds – ripe, peppery, and heartwarming – and it pops up all over the South of France, too. Australia makes terrific Shiraz, spicy and dense, with chocolatey depths, and it's also catching on elsewhere.

This is "comfort wine",
best drunk on a freezing-cold winter's evening with a gut-busting, peppery stew, or gulped at moments of sheer misery to gladden the heart.

Quality rating
Four to ten out of ten.

Fashion statement
Was rarely recognized. Now everyone wants it.

Another batch of reds: Don't miss a good glug of GRENACHE (or Garnacha, as the Spanish know it), for a likeable, no-nonsense mouthful of sweetly ripe, red fruit, mainly berries and plums, with herby hints. Swig it at a barbecue. SANGIOVESE is an Italian specialty, the greatest grape in Tuscany, and chiefly responsible for Chianti. Think slightly sour cherries and strawberries, a subtle note of tea-leaf and thyme.

TEMPRANILLO is the finest Spanish grape, the main man behind Rioja, where it's aged in new oak barrels for years until it emerges mellow and soft with tones of creamy vanilla and strawberry perfume. Then there's MALBEC (concentrated, rounded, black cherries), at its best from Argentina.

Finally, Z is for ZINFANDEL. Move up from bland, pale-pink versions and head for the wonderful, dark, raspberry- and pepper-tinged reds that represent California wine at its best.

Sparkling wine

Want some extra fizz in your life? Then here's the low-down: CHAMPAGNE is only called Champagne when it comes from, er, Champagne. This small area of northeast France makes all of it, from a blend of Chardonnay,

Pinot Noir, and Pinot Meunier grapes. Or sometimes just from Chardonnay (*blanc de blancs*) or just the two others (*blanc de noirs*). The very best Champagnes in the world are heavenly (but GET that price tag!), whereas the cheapest (still not very cheap) are an acid trip, and as much fun as smooching with an unripe lemon.

If you can't afford the good stuff, or at least the medium-priced stuff, you'll be better off with a fine sparkling wine from New Zealand, California or Australia; or try a French fizz that says *crémant* on the label as these are the next best after champers.

For bubbles on a budget, CAVA is a must. Thank you, Spain, for providing a fresh, snappy sparkler at a price mere mortals can afford. For the record, it's made in the same time-consuming way as Champagne, but from local Spanish grape varieties, which must cost zip per ton. Or they don't pay the workers. Whatever, just be grateful. Cava isn't particularly complex, deep, or meaningful, but it IS fun fizz, perfect for parties/cheap celebrations/mixing with OJ or cassis to make cocktails/seducing someone who isn't quite worth Champagne. Italian prosecco is a good alternative.

Choose brut
for a dry, refreshing style.

Sweeter fizz
is meant to go with desserts, cakes, and Auntie's tea-party.

Always chill fizz well before serving,
warm bubbles should be found only in the bath.

Stronger stuff

A quick word in your ear about SHERRY and PORT. I'm whispering it: they're great. Honestly. You might think they're fantastically outdated, like something whiskery colonels sipped while they ran the British Empire (and come to think of it, they did). Clergymen and grannies like them, too – but never mind that. They deserve the attention of a super-modern, twenty-first century chick.

Dry pale sherry (*fino* or *manzanilla* on a bottle tells you it's dry) is so tangy, lemony, zingy, zappy, and all-round refreshing that it is without doubt the world's greatest aperitif. It wakes up your whole mouth and gets you in the mood for food.

Serve chilled and fresh
with salty snacks.

Other sherry styles include medium, amber-coloured, and nutty ones (*amontillado*), and even darker, nuttier, sometimes sweeter concoctions (*oloroso*).

Sip with
cheeses, nuts or meaty soups.

Port, from the hot, dry Douro Valley in Portugal, is another versatile fortified wine (i.e. wine with extra added spirit – watch those alcohol levels). Although some sickly ports exist (avoid cheap "ruby"), it can be dazzlingly wonderful, especially if you get your sticky paws on a mature vintage port. Vintage ports are only released in good years, about three times a decade.

Try late bottled vintage port for a cheaper version from less-than-brilliant years – they're easier to drink when young. And don't miss aged tawny port, as it's one of the best drinks in the whole wide world.

Serve tawny chilled
with chocolate desserts for serious self-indulgence.

*Like shopping for lipstick

Now that you know more about the styles of wine that are out there, it's time to go and get 'em. Here's where we look at the best places to buy wine, and how to spot a bargain. Come on, girls: let's hit the shops!

How, where, and what to buy

Once upon a wine time, on a Saturday dad drove to a special shop. It was a hushed place, old-fashioned, and tobacco-stained, where there was a nice man who spoke in whispers. It was a traditional wine merchant. Dad chose his bottles: Spanish Rioja for Sunday lunch, Liebfraumilch for mum, and a bottle of vermouth for Aunt Gladys. Everyone pretended to like them.

Those days are long gone. Now it's we females who are more likely to buy wine. That's because today, depending on where you live, wine is picked up along with the rest of the weekly shopping. It's not a special purchase; it's just another thing on the list, so we sling it in along with the soap, the salad, and the steak. (If you live in the US best skip to the next page.)

Although it's great that wine is now so easy to buy, and it's nothing short of wonderful that Dad now lets us choose it, you have to agree that this is kind of a soulless way to go about it. Shopping for wine should be fun, interesting – exciting, even! Like shopping for clothes or a decent novel. That said, here's what's good about shopping in BIG STORES:

Convenience
Nice 'n' easy, isn't it, to get your wine WITH the food you're planning to cook on Saturday night?

Good value
Economies of scale mean cheaper wines, and big stores usually have impressive special offers. Especially recommended for cheap, everyday drinking (although expect lots of bland big brands).

Fast turnover
Which means fresher, newer wines.

One potential problem, though, can be the staff. Try going up to some assistants and asking if you should buy the Gevrey-Chambertin to match your roast duck tonight.

Do you think they will: a) smile delightedly, grasp your hand, and rush you across the aisle towards the bottle of your dreams? Or b) look dumbfounded, and point you in the vague direction of the discount cat food? I think we all know the answer to that.

This is where the TRADITIONAL MERCHANT still comes in very handy. Good things about buying wine this way:

You get to try

different, rarer wines, sometimes sourced from winemakers who can't supply the big shops.

The staff members

are (or should be) more wine-wise and can help you find out a lot more about the bottles you buy.

If you become a regular

they will tip you off on end-of-line sales, new vintage releases, special offers, local winemaker talks, etc. In short, you will become more of a wine buff.

If you go to a merchant, ask to try something (you never know when you're going to get lucky...), or at least get the friendly person behind the counter to describe the flavours and aromas of the wine and tell you which food or occasion he or she would match it to.

All in all, treat it like buying expensive cosmetics: you want personal service, you want to try it out, and you want to feel you're spoiling yourself rotten.

Three other interesting ways to buy wine:

By mail order

Seeing that wine is a heavy, awkward thing to buy in bulk and get home, let alone up the stairs or to the top of your high-rise, why not have it delivered to your front door? There are plenty of good mail-order firms around; go for one with an informative, appealing brochure with sensible tasting notes and tempting special offers. Grill them about the wine over the phone if you have any doubts. Oh, and pick a well-established company, too, since there are always some dubious types around.

The internet

This is a relatively new way to shop for wine, of course, but there are some good companies out there with enticing websites full of pertinent info and mouthwatering tasting notes. Again, go for a company with a decent track record. And beware of delays: some promise a faster service than they can deliver. Don't order your wedding wine from lazeebooze.com.

Cellar door

The very best way. Go to the winery door, sample the wines, buy at (most likely) the best prices, and know that the wines have been stored well and opened at around the right time. Also, visiting wineries is a truly great way to spend your time. You'll pick up a sense of the culture and history surrounding the wine region; you may meet the purple-handed winemaker; and you might even ruffle the leaves of the vines that produced your wine. Nice, huh?

The price is right

We all love a bargain, but how do you spot one in liquid form? It's tricky. We're not talking about something uniform here, like paper towels. Wine varies so much from bottle to bottle that it's impossible to generalize. But it IS possible to make an educated guess – so here is a simple list of a few wine styles that usually offer value for money, followed by a few that most certainly DO NOT. Warning: there will be a few exceptions, so please don't take the following as gospel. Look, too, for special offers from outlets you trust – "bin-end" offers (leftover bottles CAN be nice, you know), and BOGOF ("buy one, get one free") deals – although only be tempted by wines you know you already like. After all, who wants to get stuck with TWO bottles of pigswill?

Here are some tips on bargain buys (some are more widely available than others):

German Riesling

not nasty, super-cheap German paint stripper, but the real McCoy that says "Riesling" on the label.

Hungary

party-pleasers, especially the dry, spicy whites.

Alsace

not dirt-cheap, but good-value, exciting, aromatic whites from this part of eastern France.

Languedoc-Roussillon

turning out fruity, modern Vin de Pays d'Oc in the deep south of France.

Cava
Spain's refreshing, reliable sparkler from the Penedès area.

Southern Italian and Sicilian reds
soft, rich, and well-rounded.

Portuguese reds
plenty of flavour and juicy ripeness for your money.

Chile
producing some of the best-value New World wines around.

But, don't touch these with a ten-foot pole:

Cheap Bordeaux
thin, dull, nothing like the fabulous Bordeaux reds further up the ladder.

"Cut-price" Champagne
lean, mean, acidic stuff that will push up your dental bill.

Basic Beaujolais/Beaujolais Nouveau
thin and jammy, so trade up to Beaujolais-Villages for better, riper flavours.

Collectors' California
ridiculous prices for the top wines from the West Coast. Yes, they're good, but not THAT good.

Applying the finishing touches

You may have chosen a brilliant bottle, BUT the wonderful world of wine is still full of potential pitfalls. So, girls, when you've come this far, don't let yourself down. A terrific serve is called for…

Bottle etiquette and minding your manners

Opening wine

Picture this: a suave, sophisticated wine waiter in a fancy restaurant with a bottle of wildly expensive Champagne to open for a scary VIP. Waiter grasps the icy bottle, twists the cork, and it pops out in his hand with an elegant "pssht". The bubbles rise gently to the brim, and the waiter pours it beautifully without spilling one precious drop before turning on his heel and exiting.

Now picture yourself in the same situation: you wrestle the slippery bottle out of the bucket and the label slides off in your hot, sweaty palms. As you grapple with the sticky mess, the cork unexpectedly explodes with a huge bang, knocking out the eye of the VIP and spraying priceless bubbly all over his guests. You burst into tears/get hysterical/wet your pants.

Can you see the difference? (There is quite a big one.) Here, in easy-to-follow steps, is how to open a bottle of sparkling wine. The following really works.

Chill it (the bottle, not you)

Cold bubbles are less likely to explode than warm bubbles – honest. It has something to do with physics.

Wrap a clean linen napkin around it

if the bottle is damp. Take off the foil capsule and wire cage, and keep one hand hovering over the cork in case it explodes. Now grasp it firmly at the base with one hand and around the top with the other.

Twist the bottle

in one direction and the cork in the other, gently easing out the latter. Aim for control, and that quiet, classy "pssht" sound. The wine is less likely to spray everywhere if you do it that way. It also helps to hold the bottle at an angle.

In comparison, opening non-sparkling wine is a piece of cake. Just find a good corkscrew, such as a pocket, lever-style "waiter's friend", rather than a useless designer one shaped like a frog. Watch out for crumbly corks: waiter's friends are best for dealing with these so you don't end up with what look like breadcrumbs floating on top of the wine.

Chilling wine

It's simple: chill all white, rosé, and sparkling wines (including the rare red sparklers). It brings out their refreshing, juicy-tangy character. A couple of hours in the fridge should do it. Or just stick your bottles outside if it's winter and you're having a party. (Not on the street, though, or you may become popular with the wrong kind of people.) Don't chill reds EXCEPT light, juicy, soft reds such as Beaujolais, or light Loire reds (Sancerre, Chinon), which are also supposed to refresh. Big, glowering, spicy, leathery reds – ones that you pair with roast meat or hunks of smelly cheese – are NOT supposed to be mouthwatering and tangy. Don't chill them; serve them at room temperature – but not too hot.

Decanting wine

Try to aerate big, hefty, tannic reds and port. But don't just pull the cork out of the wine an hour or two before dinner; it won't make much difference. Instead, pour the liquid into a large glass decanter, letting lots of air into it, mellowing it, and expanding its aroma and flavour. If you have a mature bottle with sediment, it helps a lot to decant it. Watch carefully towards the end of pouring for the sediment at the bottom to start trickling out, then stop abruptly, and dump the gunky, granular stuff down the drain. Or into the stew (seriously), or into your ex's ear (not seriously).

Pronunciation

It's clearly embarrassing to ramble on about wine while getting the pronunciation completely wrong. Like saying "Roger" for Rioja, or "Polly-Foam" for Pouilly-Fumé. Here's a brief guide to pronouncing the most frequently messed-up winey words:

Beaujolais: bow-jo-lay

Brouilly: brew-ee

Chianti: key-anti

Gevrey-Chambertin: jevree-chambert-an

Languedoc-Roussillon: longuh-dock-roo-see-on

Meursault: mare-so

Neusiedlersee: noy-zeed-ler-zay

Pouilly-Fumé: poo-ee-foom-ay

Puligny-Montrachet: poo-li-nee-mon-rash-ay

Recioto: reh-chee-oto

Rías Baixas: ree-ahss bi-shahss

Rioja: ree-och-ah

Sémillon: semi-yon

Spätlese: shpate-laze-uh

Viognier: vee-on-yeh!

Yquem: ee-kem

Qualitätswein bestimmter Anbaugebiete: oh-for-get-it

You can tell a lot about the opposite sex by watching what they drink. Here's how to identify six different types of male by their choice of wine. Warning: you almost certainly know at least one of these men…

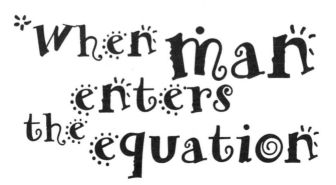

*When man enters the equation

His wine choice =
his personality

Bubbly Barnaby

Barnaby works in journalism, publishing or the upper echelons of PR, and you'll meet him at a gallery opening, a highbrow book launch, or any sophisticated soirée where the canapés are frilly and the fizz flows. He's snobby and aristocratic (which might mean he has money), but has bohemian pretentions (so he might not). He may seem other-worldly – but just watch the way he plies the girls with the bubbly stuff.

Barnaby turns up, usually on a work freebie, at all the season's most desirable events, and often wangles a box at the opera. His great love (apart from the arts and himself) is fine vintage fizz, especially Dom Pérignon (he calls it "DP"), Bollinger ("Bolly") and Krug (er, "Krug"). At first, he appears glamorous, romancing you with candlelit dinners, poetry readings, and obscure black-and-white films. This soon pales as you discover he's not the slightest bit bubbly by nature, but tortured and self-pitying, especially when drunk on Champagne (or absinthe, which it turns out he's addicted to).

Verdict

Any floppy-haired, arty type who sidles up fingering his flute is probably best avoided.

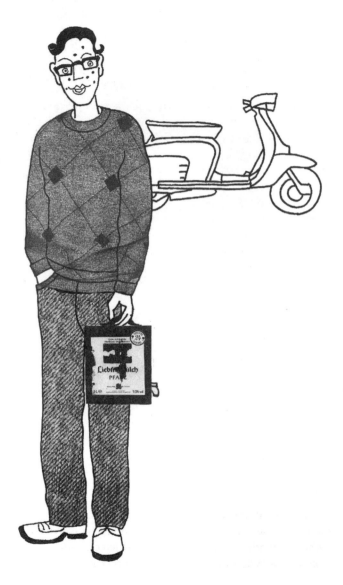

Liebfraumilch Linus

Linus has an inkling that he won't get a girl on looks alone, so he decides to go for the "best-friend" approach, then lunges after he's gained her confidence. This isn't just a horrible, creepy way to score with someone; it's bound to end in failure. You get together at an evening course in flower arranging, which Linus has joined just so he can meet the opposite sex. He's clearly a nerd, but might be kind of sweet. He thinks you're super because you glanced at him over the gladioli while wearing a nice blouse. He informs you that one of his other hobbies is wine appreciation and invites you to his frighteningly neat basement apartment to taste his range.

Convinced that he knows the perfect drinks for ladies, he stocks up on bland, non-descript whites, serving them warm in stingy sherry glasses, perhaps adding a touch of soda for a spritzer, and if he really likes you, a stuffed olive. His come-on is totally unexpected and almost as revolting as his wine. Still, he seems fine about being rejected, especially after you've thrown up noisily in his bathroom. And once you've cleared up the misunderstanding, you join his legion of steadfast female friends. Not.

Verdict

Possibly worth introducing to an equally desperate friend – if she likes him, they are bound to be married within a month. At least you won't get jealous and wonder why you never snapped him up yourself.

Claret Clarence

Stockbroker Clarence thinks wine should be taken very seriously indeed – as something to make money from. He regularly buys loads of the finest red Bordeaux, burgundy, and vintage port, but he rarely drinks it. Instead, he stashes it away in a dark cellar, talks endlessly about its value, and eventually sells it for a profit, usually at auction. All of which makes him brain-numbingly dull: a wine connoisseur from hell. After all, wine is supposed to be drunk and enjoyed, but Clarence simply sees it as another asset. At least you can guarantee he'll order something fabulously pricey and famous at a restaurant (his bonus was good this year), and you will get to drink most of it.

He, meanwhile, will swill it around his mouth and rattle on about the various merits of the year, the château, the points Parker gave it (*who?*), and the reserve release versus the second label (*what?*). The most excited he ever gets, in or out of bed, is when a really cult wine comes his way – its current worth almost rivals the money he has made on his yacht! He takes you to dinner, bores you into oblivion, and never calls you again because you describe the mature Puligny-Montrachet he orders as "quite nice". Still, that tip he gave you about the Château Latour paid off.

Verdict

Not for you. Not for anyone worth knowing. Find a man who thinks wine is a great, life-enhancing DRINK.

Shiraz Steve

Steve loves life – especially girls and football, rugby and beer, and beer and beer... Oh, and red wine, too. Preferably big, boisterous, no-nonsense Australian Shiraz, swigged from the bottle at a barbecue. Man's food, man's wine. He might go for a Rioja or a South African Pinotage, or even a whacking-great, lip-staining Californian Zinfandel – somehow they sound macho enough. You meet at a friend's summer party, where Steve is grilling enormous slabs of meat and getting increasingly smoky and sunburned. He's wearing a rugby shirt, and you can't help but admire his hearty, outdoors attitude to life.

He invites you to a sports bar and drinks three bottles of cheap, cheerful New World red and a bucket of beer, ordering the "Bronco-Burger" mega-special, extra fries with ketchup, and two vanilla-fudge cheesecakes. It's around then that you realize he might have a drink and diet problem. Yep, despite all Steve's sporty enthusiasm, his own exercise is limited to raising his glass and fork to his mouth. Several years later you bump into him at Weight Watchers. He's still a nice guy, but by then his triple bypass makes him an unsafe target for seduction.

Verdict

A good bloke, but it's hard to say anything interesting, let alone get romantic, with a mouthful of carbonized meat. So to speak.

Petulant Pete

Pete has got a problem – a REAL problem – with wine buffs. A regular guy except for the huge chip on his shoulder, he cannot stand the "stuck-up jerks" who go on and on about fine wine. According to Pete, they're boring and pointless. Actually, *Pete* goes on and on about wine. Wine, he complains to anyone who'll listen, is just a drink made from grapes. It doesn't taste like anything *but* grapes, and it's just "totally stupid" to pretend that there's more to it. That's his excuse, anyway, for buying all the bargain-basement bottles he can get his hands on. Any old pigswill masquerading as wine will be Pete's favourite tipple, as long as it's cheap.

French wine is "for snobs". Australian and Californian bottles are "way overpriced". He can't understand why he can no longer get hold of the dire Spanish house red he drank on the Costa Brava in 1983 – now that was a bargain, even if it did come in re-used diesel cans. Thankfully, Pete isn't after you, but he does want to date your mother, and thinks he can romance her with huge screw cap bottles of pink Lambrusco, carafes of Cypriot Crème fortified wine, and insipid German antifreeze, plus, of course, plastic flowers and cheap chocolates. Will your dear mama, who has been divorced for twenty years, fall for him? You bet.

Verdict

Bad luck. You'll drink Pete's vinous offerings whenever you go home. And it's cut-price Asti at the wedding.

Merlot Marco

Wow! This guy is sexy, if a little too swivel-hipped.
He's got everything: a successful business career, sharp
suits, flashy car, his own lizard-skin and platinum
corkscrew. And of course, lots of lovely "lay-deeez".
Marco spends much of his time flying between Europe
and the US, making it to meetings in Milan, Paris, LA,
and New York. While dining in some of the finest, and
– far more importantly – most fashionable restaurants
in the world, he has developed a picky palate and only
drinks the trendiest wines of the moment.

Actually, he doesn't care one bit what they taste like;
he just wants the international model at the next
table to notice that he has ordered a magnum of cult
California red Big Boy. You know, the legendary $2,000
Merlot that comes in its own satin-lined silver box,
made at the Napa Valley winery jointly owned by
several Hollywood heartthrobs? So how do you get
to meet Marco? You don't. Face it: he wouldn't give
you the dregs from his (gold-plated Fabergé) spittoon.
The good news is you're not missing a thing. He's vain,
materialistic, utterly shallow. Still, it would have been
nice to find out for yourself while sampling his Big Boy.

Verdict

Men like Marco are the reason why overrated wines
become cult favourites and then cost a ridiculous
amount. They are also the reason many beautiful
women remain single.

Your glass,

What a girl drinks can say a lot about her personality, too. Here are six women with very different approaches to the subject of wine – none of them entirely sane. A bit like real life, then…

your choice

Her wine choice =

her personality

Champagne Charlotte

Charlotte isn't exactly that old cliché, the Champagne Charlie – she's a female version, and one of a rapidly growing breed. It's now the girls, rather than boys, who bray into their bubbly at parties, acting like the world owes them a living (or it would, if Daddy hadn't fixed that all up). She only ever drinks Champagne, with a little Bordeaux and Chablis at dinner. She is generally found hanging around big country houses eyeing the party guests for potential husband material while servants top up her glass.

If you push her, she'll admit she doesn't know anything about wine, and doesn't even really like it, especially Champagne. So why is she drinking it? She has no idea, and in fact has very few opinions on anything except horses. It's all rather pitiful – I mean, what a waste of fine fizz! Charlotte is destined to marry a rich, dull, offensively right-wing banker who thinks she adores Champagne and keeps buying copious supplies for her. It's not until much later that she joins a wine-appreciation course and discovers she prefers warm Asti, mixing it with cola and Tabasco on occasion. When she comes out about her new tastes, her entire family and all her friends disown her.

Verdict

Needs several weeks of being forced to drink paint-stripper to appreciate what she's got.

Burgundy Belinda

Belinda loves red burgundy. She has read that it is sexy, ripe, juicy, and classy – a bit like her (except the classy part). She also adores Merlot, Zinfandel, Cabernet, those great-value Chilean reds, something from the South of France, perhaps, Spanish Rioja, South African Pinotage – oh, and those cheapies from Eastern Europe will do nicely, too. You get the picture. Belinda drinks red wine. *Any* red wine, although she likes burgundy most of all. She's ideal best-friend material, not just because she's a real laugh, a good confidante, and a genuinely warm person, but because she drinks more than you do, which is comforting.

She also has a disastrous love life, which leads to hilarious stories of red-wine-fuelled dates from hell. Her lipstick is always astray, her teeth are black, and she has a remarkable capacity for spilling everything – food *and* wine – all over your new cream carpet. After an evening of girly gossip at your place, it is at least 2AM and you invariably have to call a cab for her. Then you have to help her into it, and then you have to lend her the fare. And you have to hire a truck to take the bottles away in the morning. But we love girls like this. Why? Let's face it: we *all* turn into Burgundy Belinda now and then.

Verdict

Makes you feel better about yourself until you realize she has straightened herself out, found a decent man, and left you flailing around on your own in a sea of red wine.

Cheapskate Kate

We might have a bit of Burgundy Belinda in us, but it can only be hoped that you, dear reader, have nothing in common with Cheapskate Kate. Especially if you're coming over to my place. Kate is irredeemably stingy, a total miser who can't bear to part with more than the bare minimum when it comes to "non-essentials" like wine (*wine? non-essential?*). You meet at the local library, where she has been appointed to collect outstanding fines. She takes half a week's wages from you, then invites herself to dinner.

Ever efficient, she turns up promptly with a gift of the most tart, mouth-puckering white wine you have ever had the misfortune to encounter. She bought it in that awful discount store around the corner where it had gathered dust and cobwebs on the bottom shelf for five years. While you pour it and watch your guests wince in pain at the high acidity levels, Kate rummages around your kitchen until she finds a bottle of extremely expensive white Bordeaux. "I hope we're going to try *this*," she cries triumphantly, cracking it open herself. At the end of the evening, you discover she has swiped your corkscrew, three CDs, a pot of basil, and a friend's husband.

Verdict

You know how people are said to look like their dogs? Kate's wine reflects her personality: thin, mean, pale, and plain nasty.

Specials

Dieting Davina

There's no getting away from it; wine contains calories. For Davina, who is determined to avoid putting such evil things in her mouth, this presents a serious dilemma. After yet another Christmas feeding frenzy, she has embarked on a strict weight-loss plan that involves an intricate system of points given for general enjoyment of life, trying to keep the score as low as possible. A slender waist, svelte legs, and utter misery are her avowed aims – and no one's going to stop her.

Unfortunately, Davina loves a glass of sweet, sticky, dessert wine (just about the worst type for dieters). What she really, *really* wants with her dry egg-white omelette is a pint of gloopy dessert wine, perhaps with a scoop of vanilla ice-cream and chocolate sprinkles floating in it. What she should go for, of course, is the occasional, sensible treat of a small glass of fine, dry German Riesling, with its naturally low alcohol level and therefore fewer calories. But Davina can't be sensible – after three deeply unhappy days of boiled lettuce shavings and celery leaves, she opts to drown in a bath of Sauternes.

Verdict

Probably a good thing Davina didn't meet Shiraz Steve. A sad case, and a reminder that wine should be drunk in moderation: not too much – or indeed, too little.

Pregnant Penny

Davina might be trying to deny herself wine, but Penny, a shy, retiring type who is seven months pregnant, simply isn't allowed any. Or is she? One of her fifteen pregnancy manuals recommends one glass a day, but seven others suggest only the odd sip, and all the rest tell her she is murdering her unborn child if she thinks fleetingly about Chardonnay. Unhelpfully, her friends each have totally different views. When Penny meekly admits that she had a small glass of white a week ago last Thursday, their reactions range from outrage to gales of laughter.

What to do? She's totally baffled, and becomes worried that she's a) getting boring, and b) getting a guilt complex, and c) getting tense, which is bad for the baby. At a girls' night out, she decides the best option is to order a lurid pink non-alcoholic cocktail that only looks like the real McCoy. Unfortunately, the security guard in the bar notices her stomach and the paper umbrella in her drink and draws the wrong conclusion. The police are called and haul her from the premises. She makes the front page of the national papers. After this little incident, Penny sticks to Perrier.

Verdict

Oh, Penny! Wine is supposed to create happiness – not a terrible guilt trip. Leave the stuff alone until you can truly enjoy it.

Vintage Victoria

Victoria is very interested in wine. Oh, very interested indeed. She is a serious student of the subject, and has all the facts at her fingertips. She is the founder of her local wine club, she carries little fine-wine pocket guides wherever she goes, and she subscribes to all the specialist magazines. She has even taken down the teen-idol posters from her bedroom and replaced them with vintage charts that tell her which years were best in Bordeaux, Burgundy or Portugal.

When she's not working, Victoria marches around the wine regions, taking it all far too seriously and even boring the winemakers she encounters with her lists of wine facts and figures. She also collects labels – soaked off in the bathtub and left to dry on blotting paper before being filed carefully away. Her other collection is autographed bottles, mostly acquired after she has slept with a famous winemaker and/or wine critic. Luckily for her, the wine world is entirely without good taste in these matters, so she scores a lot. You meet Victoria at a wine-appreciation class, where, unfortunately, she sits next to you, spitting with great aplomb into a plastic cup. It is weeks before you realize that she's teetotal.

Verdict

Victoria seems to have got the whole subject of wine upside down. Not the facts, of course, but the enjoyment side of it. As in, the part where you actually *drink* the stuff.

Winemakers are sexy beasts, the rock stars of the industry, right? Wrong. Here's what they are *really* like. And for any girl who wants to BE one rather than DO one, here's what it takes.

The Midas touch*

Old World

Winemakers:

New World

a breed apart

Sometimes the world of wine seems full of contradictions. Take winemakers, for example. More specifically, one from a

New World wine area:
Australia, New Zealand, California, South Africa, and so on.

The typical New World winery may be a modern, high-tech, laboratory-type of place, squeaky-clean and super-hygienic, but, in my experience, the average guy who works there is anything but.

Hairy, grimy, fat, and unkempt, a typical New World winemaker is the antithesis of his wine. He may spend every spare moment scrubbing down his stainless-steel fermentation vats or his barrels, but he hasn't turned a shower on himself in years. He's probably got a smelly dog at his heel or some mangy, stick-thin winery cat that gets its kicks out of eating snakes in the vineyard. He may sleep on rags on the winery floor. It's all very unpleasant.

Until he opens a bottle or two.

Fact:
the more unsavoury the winemaker, the better the wine. All his efforts have gone into his craft.

If you visit a state-of-the-art winery in, say, Santa Cruz or Barossa Valley, and a sweaty, whiskery guy in hob-nailed boots greets you, scratching his crotch and kicking his mutt, then get ready – you are in for a treat. No, the WINES, stupid! They will be wonderful.

He would have lovely, old-fashioned manners and treat you like the "lay-dee" you are

Then

there's the Old World winemaker.

Although things have improved of late, time was when cheaper European wines had a well-deserved reputation for being thoroughly unreliable. Bottles from France, Spain, Italy, and Portugal were often grubby, musty, rough, and rustic – dirty, somehow.

By contrast, the winemaker was always impeccably turned out, attired in tweed, with a natty bow tie, a twiddly little moustache *à la* Hercule Poirot, and a clean whiff of eau de toilette. He would have lovely, old-fashioned manners and treat you like the "lay-dee" you are. Sadly, he would also show you a rank barrel room full of rats and cobwebs and reveal a selection of foul-tasting liquids.

Plus, if he came from Iberia or Italy, he'd chain-smoke while you sampled the wines (not such a bad thing with bottles like these). At least he'd take you off to a fancy restaurant for a fabulous lunch (whereas the New World guy would simply hurl an old 'roo bone in your direction).

Winemakers now fly in and out of just about every country, so today you might meet Mr Hairy in the South of France, or encounter Monsieur Poirot in South Africa. But it's still true to say that some of the finest and most interesting winemakers (and, when you get to know them, the best guys all round) are the least promising on first introduction.

Don't ever fall for a winemaker

Then there's a new breed of intellectuals. They look like college professors, all brainy and square and briefcase-carrying. They are fascinated by granite/schist soil types or canopy management (that's cutting leaves to let the sun in – wowee). They always make wine from the grapes of just one tiny plot of land, so they can study its geography in mind-boggling detail. They fly the world giving worthy but mind-numbingly boring seminars on irrigation or pest control. They are also likely to be interested in organic viticulture (going without the usual sprays and artificial fertilizers) or its more controversial cousin, biodynamics, which involves observing the planets for their influence on the vines, treating the grapes homeopathically, and burying cow horns in the vineyards. Seriously.

Don't ever fall for a winemaker (not that the above would make you want to). For one thing, even if they don't tell you straightaway, it turns out that they are

ALWAYS married, and have been since about the age of twelve. To a childhood sweetheart. Who is the daughter of another winemaker. And they always have loads of small children. I don't know what it is about the wine world, but it seems more family-focused than *The Waltons*. Even if they get divorced, the winemaker usually gets married again (to another family friend) within about ten minutes and has another five kids.

Women winemakers are a different kettle of fish. You don't get any neatly turned-out, smiley, air-kissy female winemakers. Thank goodness. They are mainly grumpy, abrupt, busy, and hassled. As such they are the least pretentious group of people in the world and well worth getting to know. When they do stop working for a moment and relax, they REALLY know how to let their hair down.

Want to be one?

It's stupendously hard work (I'm told). You spend years at a wine college studying and all your spare time trying to earn the fees for the course, or helping out at a winery.

Believe me, I know about helping out in wineries. It means endless cleaning of everything in sight, being almost permanently soaked to the skin, and putting up with the characters described above. And you have to be strong and brave: try lifting a big pitchfork of grapes, upending a barrel or wrestling a snake in the vineyard. I worked briefly at a winery in South Australia about eight years ago, and as a small, weedy girlie was shamed after about five minutes and sent to clean stainless-steel vats for the next six weeks. Fun.

*Slip into something

When it comes to matters of love, it must never be forgotten that alcohol can be your greatest asset OR your worst enemy. It's true: drink a little wine and your love life may be hugely improved. Drink a lot of wine and it could ruin your ENTIRE LIFE, leaving you a sad, bitter, old lush left on her own FOREVER. Here's why...

more comfortable

and wine require
juggling

First date
(at a party)

You want to:

Look perfect, down to the last curled eyelash. Waft around a delicious, subtle, expensive scent. Make witty, informed conversation. Be at all times mysterious, beguiling, enigmatic.

Drink Far Too Much (DFTM), and instead, you:

Turn crimson, especially in the eyes. Acquire a gunky, red-wine-and-lipstick tide mark around your mouth. Smell like a bar at dawn. Cackle like a hag. Drool.

Solution

Don't

drink half a bottle while getting ready.

Wear

more perfume.

Don't

let your bottom jaw hang loose.

Look:

just don't overdo it, OK?

Wine choice

Best option

A sophisticated Tuscan red.

Worst option

Hungarian Bull's Blood.

Second date
(eating out)

You want to:

Go for a sophisticated dinner. Elegantly sip a tall flute of fizz. Converse with the waiter and generally impress. Pick delicately at a salad, a fish main course, and some fruit to finish.

DFTM, and instead, you:

Order a disgustingly sweet cocktail. Champagne with anchovies brings on vinegary hiccups. Horrible red wine with rare warthog steak followed by port and brandy with smelly cheeses = nausea. Food- and wine-stained teeth/dress/tablecloth. Halitosis.

Solution

Stick

to dry white wine only.

Pick light dishes

so that you're not tempted by blockbuster reds/port.

For once,

let the waiter be a chauvinist pig. Get him next time you're in.

Wine choice

Best option

Fine Chablis, relatively light and refreshing, served chilled in an ice bucket.

Worst option

Sickly, cheap, ruby port.

Glow, dazzle, beam, simper

The Wedding

You want to:

Look picture-perfect. Glow, dazzle, beam, simper.
Generally act like Snow White on a particularly good
day. Fit into your slim-line ivory dress with room
to spare. Look lovingly at the groom, adore friends
and family, and be utterly bewitching throughout
the ceremony and reception.

DFTM, and instead, you:

Stagger up the aisle, leaning clumsily on father.
Slur vows. Burst out of dress during first dance.
Throw pink-faced fit at hateful relations, fall over,
and cry. Grab the best man behind the marquee.
All captured on video.

Solution

This is the ONE day

when it is extremely advisable to sip just one glass of
good Champagne until late in the proceedings. Do the
big-drinking thing on the girl's night out instead.

Wine choice

Best option

Vintage Champagne of suitable maturity: soft, yeasty,
and simply oozing class.

Worst option

Sangria made with dirt-cheap Spanish vino,
decorated with maraschino cherries.

The fight

You want to:

Win. Be clever. Win. Show him up for how wrong he is.
Prove a point. Win. Make up ecstatically, get your own
way, and make him feel bad all at the same time. Gain
a new respect from him. Make him say, "You look
beautiful when you're angry."

DFTM, and instead, you:
(*See* "the break-up", p.97.)

Solution
Drink with care:
> slowly does it.

While sipping,
> think up brilliant new strategy.

Wine choice
Best option
> Spine-tingling, ice-cold Riesling, refreshing with
> rapier-sharp acidity and naturally low in alcohol.

Worst option
> Buckets of sickly, feeble rosé – or any wine
> for wusses.

The break-up

You want to:

Be dignified, wounded yet determined, heartbroken yet strong. Look particularly lovely as you walk away.

DFTM, and instead, you:

Become screeching witch waving bottle, spitting and furious. Lie prone in horrible heap, skirt around ears, cursing and ranting as he leaves.

Solution

Never resort to

cheap spirits.

Once he's gone,

open your BEST wine and celebrate with a good friend (or, even better, the next conquest. If successful, go back to start of chapter and repeat process).

Wine choice

Best option

Assertive, powerful, brassy New World Chardonnay.

Worst option

Not wine, but a bottle of cut-price vodka.

And finally: I almost forgot "The Sex". And that's exactly the problem. If you DFTM, you hardly remember sex at all. What you can recall is a deeply unromantic, short moment of fumbling, mumbling, and bungling. Yes, it *was* that bad. And no: you won't be seeing him again.

*Smooth operator

How far should you go
to find exactly the right bottle
to match with a specific dish?
When does this quest start to
look pathetic? Plus: how to
demystify restaurant wine lists.

Right food,
right wine —
simple every time

Whole books, whole magazines, whole LIVES have been devoted to the subject of finding the perfect wine to go with a particular dish. Isn't that unbelievably sad? Some wild-eyed fanatic samples 800 dry, aromatic whites to pinpoint the exact one that goes with salmon en croute, and yet there are people all over the world happily washing down the wretched fish with a rich red.

do grasp a few teensy-weensy facts about food and wine pairing

This is the problem with "rules" about wine and food matching. You become unhappy with those make-do, incorrect pairings that, up until you read the "rules", you actually liked very much. Dare to learn more about this subject, and when someone brings a leathery, red Bordeaux to go with your special grilled squid, you could turn into a homicidal maniac. So, you've been warned: don't delve too deeply into this dangerous, addictive subject.

Still, if you've spent all week preparing a gourmet Christmas dinner with all the trimmings, then finding the right type of wine *does* matter. It's fine to ignore the lunatics, but do grasp a few teensy-weensy facts about food and wine pairing.

DON'T worry about the COLOUR of the wine,

but **DO** think about its richness or lightness. A mild-mannered, soft red goes well with a meaty fish like salmon, while a loud, brassy Chardonnay isn't bad with some meats such as pork or even steak. It's a balancing act – not an exercise in colour coordination.

DO consider sweetness/dryness levels

A tart, bone-dry wine is about as much fun with crème brûlée as a mouthful of vinegar. And a sickly sweet sparkler as an aperitif with salty snacks is just plain nasty. Try to match sweet-tasting food (including sweetish seafood) with sweeter wines, and salty, tart dishes with dry wines.

DO think about the other ingredients on the plate

Chicken in a light lemon sauce is very different to curried chicken, say, and demands an entirely different wine. Add a vinaigrette dressing, or melted butter or a cream sauce to fresh vegetables and you'll need to pick a new wine each time.

DO look at the sauces

that go with your dish and go for wine with the same character. Lemon goes with grilled white fish, so choose a lemony wine; red-berry sauces suit turkey, so opt for a juicy red with cherry and cranberry flavours; mint complements lamb, so pick a minty Cabernet. Geddit?

There are some almost impossible ingredients that clash with ninety-nine per cent of the wines in the world. Asparagus, artichokes, fluffy egg dishes, plain chocolate, vinaigrette-dressed tomatoes... I recently ordered quails' eggs with Champagne in a fancy restaurant, only realizing they were pickled when I bit into one. Bummer: the Champagne was ruined. So be aware that some dishes are decidedly *not* wine friendly. The best matches are:

Asparagus

Light Chablis or dry Muscat.

Eggs (not pickled)

Neutral, unoaked, dry whites.

Bitter chocolate

Sweet Muscats, or chilled tawny port.

Vinaigrette

Grassy Sauvignon Blanc or similar light, crisp, unoaked white.

Raw tomatoes

Fresh, cold Sauvignon Blanc.

And...

Pickled eggs

Cold beer.

Now for the not-so-tricky. Some great matches are:

Salty snacks like olives and nuts
Fino sherry.

Shellfish and seafood
Sauvignon Blanc or good Muscadet.

Goats' cheese
Sancerre.

Roast lamb
Claret (red Bordeaux).

Roquefort
Sauternes.

Onion tart and quiche
Pinot Blanc.

Smoked salmon
New World Chardonnay.

Red, peppery stews
Australian Shiraz.

Wedding cake
and plum pudding
Cold sweet bubbly.

Restaurant wine lists

Apply all the rules already mentioned to choosing wine in restaurants. Also apply a healthy dash of self-confidence. Many normally gutsy, ambitious women fall to pieces when presented with a wine list and a condescending (male) waiter. Why? We wouldn't cringe with self-doubt in a shoe shop or when buying a car – so what's wrong with wine?

The most important thing you can do to get a good wine is to make that waiter work. Ask him as many questions as it takes to get a bottle that suits you and your food. Make him bring you a little taster if you're not convinced. And certainly make him replace any bottle that seems sub-standard or different from its billing. You wouldn't eat a dish that was seriously wrong in some way, would you? (Please, please say no.) So send back that dud wine! Demand a replacement, shout loudly, and generally make the sort of hideous scene that your uncle does on special family eating-out occasions. You know, the ones where he reduces the waiter, the manager, and your mother to tears? You can do that, too! Go, sister! More seriously...

Avoid house wine

With the odd wonderful exception, they are nearly always appalling: the crappy, cheap one for gullible people out there. That's why the waiter sniggers in a sinister way when you order it. Trade up.

Finally, when in a restaurant, be on the look-out for:

Light, aromatic whites, rosés, and fizz past their prime

These wines should be from a very recent vintage or they will taste tired and dull.

Warm whites and warmer reds

Demand an ice-bucket to chill them down.

Waiters who put your wine just out of arm's reach

And then don't top up your glass themselves. It's *your* wine – grab it and serve yourself.

Interesting sherries, ports, and dessert wines

It's well worth trying unusual wines by the glass instead of ordering yet another bottle of that gruesome house red.

You wouldn't eat a dish that was seriously wrong in some way, would you?

Corked wine

Wine that smells and tastes of mushrooms and damp cardboard could be corked: send it back!

Girl power

Party, party! This is all about wine and people, mostly wine and women: girls' nights out and girls' nights in. But there's also stuff on parties with men and old people, too.

get ready to party!

When the
girls get together

When women meet up nowadays, it's usually over a glass or ten of wine. They meet in wine bars, or they go out for a meal with wine, or they head over to each other's houses armed with wine. This is a new phenomenon that has been around only since the days of Women's Wine Lib (WWL). Before WWL, in the '60s, women weren't allowed to choose or buy their own wine, and they certainly weren't allowed to drink any with their girlfriends – just the odd sip of something pale, sweet, and dull at Henry's boss' dinner party. Women who were caught together socializing with a bottle of Rioja on a ladies' night out were arrested and shipped to Australia where it was OK to drink wine.

Before WWL, in the '60s, women weren't allowed to choose or buy their own wine

It makes you wonder what women did on a girls' evening out pre-1965. Oh, yes: Tupperware parties. Perhaps they brought along a few tea-bags. Anyway, I'm glad I live now. Today, you can throw caution to the wind. There isn't even the pressure of a date, so a fairly cheap and cheerful bottle should be OK. That said, there are still a few types of wine that should be considered a no-no when having a girls' night in or out.

These include:

Liebfraumilch

It's not just bland and boring; Germany's weedy,
cheap white is also fantastically unfashionable.
And the sort of thing very old, if not dead, people
drink. The only girl you should be drinking this with
is your granny (who is preferably alive).

Blush Lambrusco

Pink gloop with a vague, and therefore pathetic,
spritzy fizz. This is almost TOO girly – and not
grown-up enough. Blush? You ought to.

Wine boxes

Imagine turning up to see a good friend for an
evening of gossip clutching a cardboard box with
a fiddly little plastic spout and a bag inside... NO!
It simply won't do.

Eastern European or Californian bargains

In big bottles with a screwcap. Need I continue?
If you think this is acceptable, get a life.

That cut-price, weirdly rubbery sparkling wine

you got on sale at the local hypermarket (discount
store). You know, the one that you can't force on
anyone, even at a New Year's Eve party? Give up!
Pour it down the drain. Or use it to kill the rats.

So what IS ideal refreshment for a fun, lively night with the girls? Don't be extravagant – you want something cheap and cheerful, with plenty of fruity flavour, or perhaps bubbles, that you can simply enjoy with or without food. Don't opt for wine that's too heavy and alcoholic, but pick a refreshing style: not too complex, not too upfront. This is wine that should slip down easily.

South African Chenin Blanc

Not expensive, easy-going, fruity, usually unoaked, medium-bodied.

French Sauvignon Blanc

A crisp, dry style; very fresh, clean, and mouthwatering.

Unoaked or lightly oaked Chardonnay

Avoid the heavy blockbusters and try something lighter (the label might actually say "unoaked").

Cava

Spain's bargain fizz isn't hugely exciting, but for the money, it gives lots of fresh, appley flavour and, of course, joyful BUBBLES!.

Light, fruity, and soft red wines

Pick Pinot Noir or a decent Beaujolais.

115

Other things it is useful to have when the girls turn up:

Snacks

They swear they're on diets before they turn up, then spend the evening scouring your kitchen for chocolate/peanuts/pretzels/etc.

Tissues

For tears and spillages.

Ashtrays

Of course, none of them smoke, wouldn't dream of it; well, maybe, once in a blue moon... cut to scene of fifteen women puffing away furiously.

Corkscrew

Might come in handy.

Items from memory lane

Terrible old photos/CDs/videos/school memorabilia.

More wine

Well, you know how the girls are...

Other parties

Very occasionally, you might find yourself socializing with men AND women, throwing a general sort of party. If the guests are all your age, then stick to the wines described in the list on p.114 (but forget the tissues, ashtrays, and so on on p.116). Remember to chill the bottles and serve straight from the fridge. Throw some packets of cheap nuts and other snacks around the place.

If, on the other hand, you are stuck in a hideous time-warp, forced to give or go to a cocktail party for your parents' generation, then bring out the wines described in the list on p.113. And don't forget to warm and oxidize the bottles nicely by placing them in a hot "drinks cabinet" in the party room (what WERE drinks cabinets FOR? Do you know anyone under sixty who has one? You DO?), or better still by decanting them into a hideous, chunky, cut-glass bauble and leaving it on a sunny window-sill to heat up.

Don't forget to chill the bottles and serve straight from the fridge

Finally, arrange the snacks in a nice pattern on special tiered stands, with dips and cocktail sticks, paper napkins to the side. (It's the way we've let the nibbles go that proves we girls have lost it as a generation.)

Time for a short wine break *

Wine contains alcohol. Too much alcohol makes you feel unwell. So here's how to avoid getting a hangover – and if it's too late, how to make yourself feel a little better… PLUS, your guide to wine and diets – and a personal view on wine and pregnancy.

Smart
drinking
— the
morning
after

Wine and hangovers

See the woman in the mirror with the red-rimmed, vampire eyes? See the smudged mascara, blotchy foundation, smeared lipstick? The grey teeth, the dull tongue, the scowling expression? She's fairly unattractive. Who is she? She is Hangover Woman: an anti-hero with not-very-special powers. Look: she goes into a telephone booth, whirls around with a pint of Champagne, and comes out transformed into.... an unholy mess.

see the smudged mascara?

We have all been Hangover Woman at least once (well, ninety-five per cent of us have). When I was eighteen, I thought I only got hangovers because I was a student, and students drink cheap, nasty wine. In my twenties, I thought it was because I was a single, crazy kind of a gal. Once past thirty, I blamed it on the fact that hangovers get worse when you're older. Currently I blame my hangovers on the baby, who wakes up early.

Don't make these basic errors. You get a hangover –
at any age – when you drink too much. The way you
avoid ever getting one is to drink nothing, or very little.
(Now, aren't you glad you bought this useful little
book?) However, there *are* ways to enjoy more than a
thimbleful of wine and suffer from a less fuzzy head.
Boringly, the top tips that your mother handed down
are still the ones that work best. So, for the record:

Never

drink on an empty stomach.

Never

drink wine and beer or wine and spirits together;
stick to white OR red all evening.

Drink

reasonably good quality wine.

Drink

half a gallon of water before you go to bed.

Wash

your underwear in milk at the end of the night.

Stand

on your head for half an hour before you go to sleep.

OK, I made the last two up, but it was getting really
dull there for a moment. And – simple, hellish fact –
the average woman cannot drink as much as the
average man without getting ill (we don't absorb
alcohol as effectively), so don't even attempt
to keep up with your beer-draining bloke.

Strange phenomenon: has anyone else noticed that sometimes you drink buckets of cheap red and feel fine the next day, while on other occasions you have one miniscule glass of white and feel dreadful for the next century? What's THAT all about? Occasionally, it's an excuse. As in: "Sorry about last night when I fell off my chair/ruined your party/made a pass at your husband; I only had one small glass of wine, there must have been something wrong with it." But occasionally it really *is* true, and probably means that the wine was totally terrible, wincingly high in acidity, made in filthy barrels, full of chemicals (*see* below) or heavily tannic – in short, it deeply disagreed with you. In these cases you are forgiven the hangover – but not your poor taste in wine.

Organics

Talking of chemicals, some people are genuinely allergic to the additives in wine. Particularly to sulphur, which is added to almost all wines as a preservative to keep them from oxidizing. If you think you are susceptible (say, if you get bad headaches or come out in a rash after one glass of wine), then try switching to organic wine. This is made from one hundred per cent organically grown grapes, i.e. no chemicals in the vineyards, and with significantly reduced levels of sulphur (at least half of normal levels). It's worth a try, although remember organic wine still contains alcohol, so this advice won't help if you down half a case in one night.

Wine and diets

Hangover Woman rarely makes an appearance when you are on a diet, for the simple reason that dieting girls equal less-drunken girls. Successful dieting girls, that is. You can't lose lots of weight by cutting back on food but continuing to glug wine like there is no tomorrow. In fact, that would be a very bad idea, since you'd be filling up with "empty calories with no nutritional benefits", as the women's magazines put it. Wine may look like a lo-cal, "lite" liquid, but because of the alcohol and sugar, it weighs in at anything from around eighty to 180 calories per small glass. Ouch, and cellulite all round! So, sadly, lots of wine is probably out if you are on a strict diet.

Avoid artificially low-alcohol or alcohol-free products

A sneaky way around this (actually only semi-cheating) is to switch to lighter dry whites – i.e. ones with naturally less alcohol and less sugar. Avoid artificially low-alcohol or alcohol-free products, as they tend to taste like the cesspools of Satan. OJ or cranberry juice is much tastier. But do try out genuine, naturally lower-calorie wines like fresh, appley German Rieslings (as low as seven per cent alcohol), or frothy Italian Asti (around five per cent). Many New World wines are a hefty 14.5 per cent alcohol, so that's quite a difference, I'm sure you'll agree.

Wine and pregnancy

The above is also good advice if you are trying to get pregnant and want to cut right back: watch those alcohol levels and switch to a lighter wine. Or stop altogether. But not if that means you can't stand the sight of your partner – you won't get pregnant as a teetotal celibate. Once you ARE pregnant, you are supposed to stop drinking altogether, according to some (in the USA), or cut right back, according to others (in the UK).

I continued to drink one glass of light white wine two or three times a week, and had a beer or two towards the end of my pregnancy. Each to her own, I say, as long as it's not excessive – and let the letters roll in. Do, please, make the most of not having a hangover for nine months; once the baby's out, you will look and feel permanently like Hangover Woman for the next eighteen years, even when you haven't touched a drop.

Hangover cures

Of course, hair of the dog (having another alcoholic drink) will make you feel better after a spectacular blow-out. Temporarily. Then the mind-numbing headache and nausea come back. A hopeless way to deal with matters, then, and frankly pretty sad.

Why do some people (i.e. men) insist on recommending DISGUSTING hangover cures, like raw egg (puke), or a fried English breakfast with extra sausage (gag), or even sex (die)? How can they come up with such things when the mere thought of a weak cup of herbal tea is enough to make you throw up?

No, the only answer is

lots of water. Oceans of it – and two painkillers, sleep, and a warm bath.

Those, plus something soothing for the stomach. I highly recommend homemade ginger tea: grate ginger root into very hot water, leave for a minute or two, then remove, sweeten with honey, and add a cleansing dash of lemon juice. It works, honestly – but it's all a bit of drag, so if you can't face it, try a can of warm, non-diet cola. Classy.

*that Friday-

Oh, for a glass of wine with the best company in the world. A night in with your feet up and only the remote control to hang on to. Here's to chilling out with the perfect bottle and the cat.

night feeling

At home

Evenings in

For some girls, the idea of an evening in alone is depressing; for others, it's bliss. It's all a matter of mind-set. A Friday night in front of the TV can be viewed as yet another sad date with the cat, with a glum session of eyebrow-tweezing the only thing to look forward to. OR you can view the same evening as a wonderful time for chilling out, eating what you want, watching something great, and (yes, you knew this was coming, because this is A Wine Guide...) the perfect moment to indulge in a fantastic bottle of wine!

At this point, let's be frank: Friday is not the best AFD*. It's the end of the working week. This is the time for serious socializing or serious vegging-out. On Fridays, I always decide I would rather have Saturday as my AFD. Then on Saturday, I usually nominate Sunday. And, etc. But you know what I mean: Friday is not the best day to be abstemious.

Men never seem to mind a night in, so let's decide to be relentlessly cheerful, too. Don the fluffy slippers and the oversized PJs. De-flea the cat and try telephoning the best friends (all out). Scrabble around until you find that week-old piece of pizza under the sofa. Now for the wine. Hurrah!

* Alcohol-Free Day

Don the fluffy slippers and the oversized PJs

This is clearly the moment to go for some comfort drinking. By this, I don't mean swigging vodka straight from the bottle and weeping hysterically; that's a different sort of comfort drinking reserved for especially dire moments and definitely not recommended.

No, I mean track down a warm, cozy, cuddly wine – something easy-drinking and satisfying, and of course, the perfect match for your furry slice of four seasons.

red Shiraz, packed with cassis

A quick lesson in comfort wines: very high-acid, ice-cold, dry whites are not heartwarming. Nor are old, leathery, tough reds; they might work well with Sunday's roast beef but they usually taste austere on their own. We're talking smooth, rounded, fruity flavours, so go for something from a warm climate, where the grapes get nice and ripe.

Australia is highly recommended for its indulgent, buttery Chardonnays and Semillons, or for fat, red Shiraz, packed with cassis, berry, and chocolate flavours. California can pull off a similar trick (try well-balanced Chardonnays, rich, peachy Viogniers or cherryish Pinots), as can South Africa and Chile, often for less money. From Europe, try mellow reds from southern Italy or southern France, or the newly yummy, concentrated table reds from Portugal's port country, the Douro.

And don't be afraid to open a sticky, honeyed, sweet wine as a comfort drink. So what if sugary gloop is out of fashion? No one can see you tonight except the cat. And cheap dessert wine goes wonderfully well with cheap chocolate, I find. Come to think of it, a Friday night in gives you the opportunity to do everything winey that you wouldn't dream of doing in front of your friends. So go for it: mix red and white to create a homemade rosé, garnish your drink with jelly beans, or try turning still white into fizz using dishwashing liquid and a straw. Hours of fun.

berry and chocolate flavours

The alternative to an evening spent in front of the TV is an evening spent in the bathtub. This is the moment to try out winetasting and most importantly, spitting like a wine pro. After all, it's not nice to start swirling, sloshing, and (especially) spitting in front of other people. So, run a nice deep bath. Get in with a bottle of fairly cheap wine – preferably white, not red, so that when you spit it into the water, it doesn't go all pink like the opening scene of *Jaws*.

Lie in the bathtub and pretend to be an accomplished winetaster, swirling the liquid around your mouth, muttering a few choice adjectives, then spitting as far down as your toes – wriggle them about and aim to hit them with a good straight stream of vino. It's nice to know that you won't get drunk doing this. (But you might smell like an old soak for days...)

13

The best-kept secrets

Now that you know what you are looking for, don't be caught out by the marketing hype, media claptrap, and general jargon that surrounds wine. Here's how to keep a clear head when parting with your money.

Jargon and the media
– when to believe
and when not to

On the bottle

It's no wonder we all love no-nonsense, decent, down-to-earth Australian wine. Not only does it taste great (well, usually), but its no-frills labels are almost as refreshing as what's inside. On a typical Aussie bottle it says something like:

Bloody Billabong. Shiraz. 1999.
Western Australia.

And you know where you are with a name like that, don't you? You don't know if the wine will be any good, but you can be fairly certain what's going on. It's an Australian Shiraz, made in the west of the country in 1999, by someone stupid enough to call it by such an unappealing brand name. End of story.

By contrast, let's look at the label on a fine German Riesling I happen to have in my wine rack.

Schloss Krackenstein. Rheingau.
Riesling. Spätlese. 1997er.
Qualitätswein mit Prädikat.
Weingut Von Trapp. Gutsabfüllung.

Now, I'm not a marketing expert, but it strikes me that this is a shade more difficult to get to grips with. Some mysteries should have been explained in chapter two, but the message is clear: if you want to untangle the intricacies of German wine (or Alsace wine, or Italian wine, burgundy, port, and Bordeaux for that matter), you'll need several enormous, scholarly tomes on the subject, or a wine course that lasts at least three years. And you still won't know if the wine inside the bottle is any good (although fine German Riesling invariably is).

That said, for all its difficulties, the German wine could well turn out to be the more interesting of the two. The message? At the end of the day, forget the label; the wine inside is what counts!

Girly-whirly pink wine with flowers all over the label

Turn the bottle around and you'll find the back label (another great tip, right?). Isn't the stuff written on back labels TERRIBLE? This is the producer's chance to impart lots of useful info on the origin and character of the wine. Instead, you get some drivel on the "eagles that fly over the vineyards which nestle in the foothills of the mountains". Apparently "the grapes gently ripen in the warm sun until they are picked". As one would hope, if they are going to be turned into wine.

Even worse than inane back labels are bottles unsubtly marketed to women. Girly-whirly pink wine with flowers all over the label; special *Cuvée des Femmes* in a "lighter style" than usual; "low-alcohol sparkling Chardonnay with added elderflower essence". It's fair to say that these types of wines are not aimed at the average macho man. Boycott them in protest. And because they're highly likely to be vile.

On the shelf

Watch out for the markers, offers, press recommendations, and other attractions that draw you towards the lighter fuel the shop can't wait to get rid of. Better to head for that quiet, unassuming bottle in the corner.

Also, it's a cunning ploy, but all the best-value bottles seem to be placed on the very bottom or very top shelves so you can't see them and can't be troubled to get them if you can. Make the effort! Stretch those calf muscles!

start drinking alcopops and your taste-buds are doomed

Most of all, be prepared to try as many different wines as you possibly can. Do not stick to the same old bottle of Château Ennui from Bore-deaux (geddit???) night after night. This way you are short-changing YOURSELF and that ain't funny. Why? Well, drinking only one style of wine – probably one that's cheap, obvious, and always on special offer – is the fastest way to get tired of wine. And we all know what happens then: you start drinking alcopops and your taste-buds are doomed.

Embrace change. Go for that unusual grape variety, that funny blend, that white from some obscure corner of Romania. Sure, you'll pick a few duds, but you'll also discover some fantastic flavours. This is THE way to find out more about wine: by tasting a lot of it!

On the front page

Should you take any notice of what wine critics say? As an independent, highly regarded wine writer, with twelve years' experience on books, magazines, and newspapers, I can honestly say "no". We just sit at home watching daytime soaps waiting for the next box of free samples to turn up. When we recommend a wine it's usually because we've just been offered a trip to the winery or because we like the look of the winemaker. Or because the back label says something nice about eagles on it. OK, that's not entirely true (I rarely watch daytime soaps). But, don't get too hung up on well-known critics. If you find one you like (critic, not wine), stick with him or her by all means. And perhaps it should be a "her". There's a theory that women make better tasters than men. It hasn't been proven, but many wine professionals swear that it's true.

It does make more sense to say that if you're female, then you're likely to have the same sort of taste-buds as other females of roughly the same age. So following the regular column of an eighty-year-old man, who happens to be a cigar-smoking old toad with a penchant for ancient Bordeaux, is perhaps not the best idea.

But if you've learned anything here, I hope it's to trust your own instincts. Try as many different wines as you can, think about the flavours, aromas, and textures you're experiencing, and build up a confidence about your own likes and dislikes. Because:

the best girl's guide to wine, at the end of the day, should be the girl herself.

Thanks to the Mitchell Beazley team: Hilary Lumsden, Yasia Williams, Yadzia Williams, Emma Rice, Jamie Ambrose, and Fiona Smith.
Thanks also to Martine Carter, Mum & Dad, and Jo Frank. And a special thanks to Ian, as ever, for all his help.